# Walking Falmouth

Dorene Sykes

A Guide to Falmouth's Best Nature Hikes

Walking Falmouth
Copyright © 2022 by Elizabeth Saito
All Rights Reserved.

No part of this publication may be reproduced, stored in a retrieval system or transmitted, in any form or by any means—electronic, mechanical, photocopying, recording, or otherwise—without prior written permission from the publisher, except for the inclusion of brief quotations in a review.

For more information on this title, or to report a textual error, contact the publisher:

Elizabeth Saito
elizabeth.saito@gmail.com

Additional copies of this book can be purchased on Amazon or at Eight Cousins bookstore in Falmouth, either in-store or through their website, eightcousins.com

ISBN: 978-0-9981768-6-4

Printed in the United States of America by IngramSpark

Cover & Interior Design by Van-garde Imagery, Inc.
Front cover photo by Clarke Morrison
Back cover photo by Lucy Helfrich

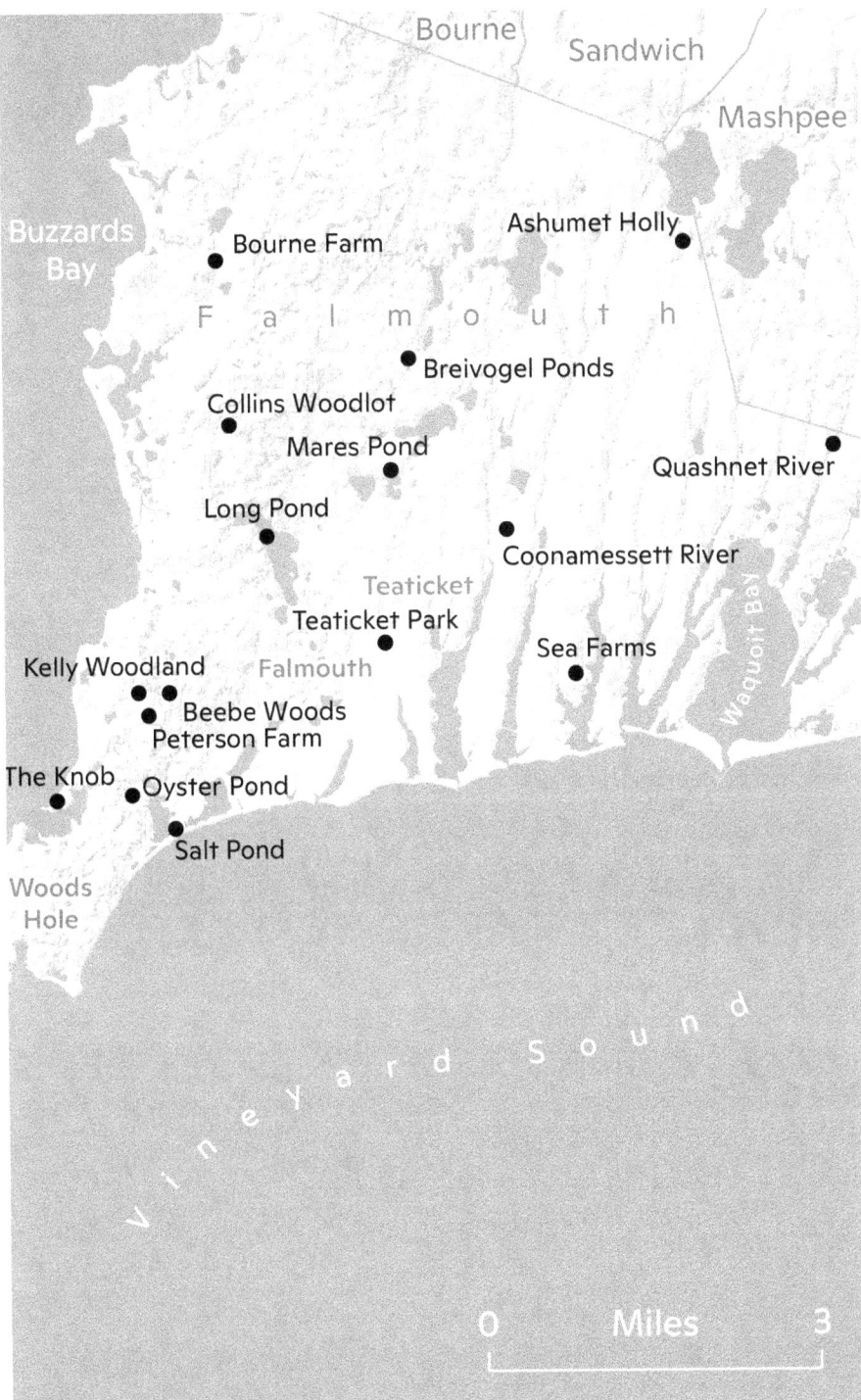

*The 300 Committee Land Trust was established in 1985 with the goal of preserving 300 acres of conservation land in Falmouth for the town's 300th birthday. The group has since preserved over 2,500 acres of open space. This book is dedicated to the founding members of The 300 Committee, most especially, Vicky Lowell, Bruce Tripp, and Eric Turkington.*

Tom Noonan

# Preface

Henry David Thoreau wrote in his essay "Walking" that "I am alarmed when it happens that I have walked a mile into the woods bodily, without getting there in spirit."

This book is a guide to the trails and history of Falmouth's conservation lands. It is also an invitation to be alert, in all seasons, to their beauty: the electric green of moss on a wet spring day, summer sunlight filtering through the forest, the autumn red of swamp maples ringed round a pond, the deep peace of the woods in winter. Nature is the spirit's universal tutor, and our intuition that we draw health and vitality from wild places is now supported by an ever-growing body of scientific research.

Thanks to the foresight and generosity of private individuals and the collective political decisions of its townspeople, 23 percent of Falmouth is permanently protected conservation land, free and open to all.

*Elizabeth Saito, Falmouth, MA, 2022*

## Acknowledgements

My sincerest thanks go to Bob Miskinis, who provided the funding for this project via the Cape Cod Foundation; Mark Chester, Dorene Sykes, and Molly and Tom Noonan, whose photographs express the beauty of these lands as words could not; Carl Churchill, whose meticulous mapmaking will ensure very few get lost; Alex Zollo for fact-checking; Molly Bang for her sharp editorial eye; and Jessica Whritenour and Lucy Helfrich of The 300 Committee for their unstinting support.

# The Hikes

Collins Woodlot . . . . . . . . . . . . . . . . . . . . . . . . . .1

The Knob . . . . . . . . . . . . . . . . . . . . . . . . . . . . . .5

Beebe Woods via Highfield Drive . . . . . . . . . . . . . . . 9

Beebe Woods via Kelly Woodland . . . . . . . . . . . . . . . 13

Coonamessett River . . . . . . . . . . . . . . . . . . . . . . . 17

Headwaters of Oyster Pond . . . . . . . . . . . . . . . . . . 21

Long Pond & Goodwill Park . . . . . . . . . . . . . . . . . . 25

Quashnet River . . . . . . . . . . . . . . . . . . . . . . . . . 29

Bourne Farm & Wing Pond Woods . . . . . . . . . . . . . . 33

Teaticket Park . . . . . . . . . . . . . . . . . . . . . . . . . . 37

Shallow Pond Woodlands & Breivogel Ponds . . . . . . . . . 41

Sea Farms Marsh . . . . . . . . . . . . . . . . . . . . . . . . 45

Ashumet Holly Wildlife Sanctuary . . . . . . . . . . . . . . .49

Salt Pond & Shining Sea Bikeway . . . . . . . . . . . . . . . 53

Mares Pond & Spectacle Pond Reservation . . . . . . . . . . 57

Peterson Farm . . . . . . . . . . . . . . . . . . . . . . . . . . 61

# The Hikes by Category

## Over Four Miles

    Beebe Woods via Highfield Drive . . . . . . . . . . . . . . . . 9

    Long Pond & Goodwill Park . . . . . . . . . . . . . . . . . . . 25

## Good for Young Children

    The Knob . . . . . . . . . . . . . . . . . . . . . . . . . . . . . . . . .5

    Headwaters of Oyster Pond . . . . . . . . . . . . . . . . . . . 21

    Teaticket Park . . . . . . . . . . . . . . . . . . . . . . . . . . . . . 37

    Ashumet Holly Wildlife Sanctuary . . . . . . . . . . . . . . .49

    Peterson Farm . . . . . . . . . . . . . . . . . . . . . . . . . . . . 61

## Accessible from the Bikepath

    The Knob . . . . . . . . . . . . . . . . . . . . . . . . . . . . . . . . .5

    Beebe Woods via Highfield Drive . . . . . . . . . . . . . . . . 9

    Headwaters of Oyster Pond . . . . . . . . . . . . . . . . . . . 21

    Long Pond & Goodwill Park . . . . . . . . . . . . . . . . . . . 25

    Bourne Farm . . . . . . . . . . . . . . . . . . . . . . . . . . . . . 33

    Salt Pond & Shining Sea Bikeway . . . . . . . . . . . . . . . 53

## Nice for a Picnic

    Beebe Woods via Highfield Drive . . . . . . . . . . . . . . . . 9

    Headwaters of Oyster Pond . . . . . . . . . . . . . . . . . . . 21

    Long Pond & Goodwill Park . . . . . . . . . . . . . . . . . . . 25

Bourne Farm . . . . . . . . . . . . . . . . . . . . . . 33

Salt Pond & Shining Sea Bikeway . . . . . . . . . . . . . . . 53

## Handicapped Accessible

Coonamessett River . . . . . . . . . . . . . . . . . . . 17

Teaticket Park . . . . . . . . . . . . . . . . . . . . . . 37

Salt Pond & Shining Sea Bikeway . . . . . . . . . . . . . . . 53

## Hunting Prohibited Year-Round

The Knob . . . . . . . . . . . . . . . . . . . . . . . . 5

Beebe Woods via Highfield Drive . . . . . . . . . . . . . . . 9

Beebe Woods via Kelly Woodland . . . . . . . . . . . . . . 13

Headwaters of Oyster Pond . . . . . . . . . . . . . . . . 21

Bourne Farm . . . . . . . . . . . . . . . . . . . . . . 33

Teaticket Park . . . . . . . . . . . . . . . . . . . . . . 37

Sea Farms Marsh . . . . . . . . . . . . . . . . . . . . 45

Ashumet Holly Wildlife Sanctuary . . . . . . . . . . . . . . 49

Salt Pond & Shining Sea Bikeway . . . . . . . . . . . . . . . 53

Peterson Farm . . . . . . . . . . . . . . . . . . . . . 61

# Important Words of Warning

## TICKS
Ticks are abundant on the Cape, and they carry Lyme disease and a variety of other illnesses. Caution and diligence will prevent tick bites. It is essential to check yourself for ticks after walking in the woods. Check your clothing immediately after a walk, and when you arrive home, take off your clothes and inspect your skin. Wearing light-colored clothing and tucking your pants into your socks will increase the likelihood of spotting a tick before it bites you. Walking on narrow trails where you brush frequently against vegetation increases your risk of being bitten, as does lying or sitting on the forest floor. Most tick-borne illnesses are treatable with antibiotics. For more information on ticks, what they look like, how to remove them, and the symptoms of tick-borne illnesses, visit cdc.gov/ticks/.

## POISON IVY
Poison ivy is ubiquitous on Cape Cod and causes a red, itchy rash on the skin. The vine grows up tree trunks and along the ground. Its green leaves grow in clusters of three, so a handy mnemonic is "Leaves of three, let it be." In spring, the leaves have a reddish shine, and in fall, they turn bright red, orange, and yellow. If you come in contact with poison ivy, wash your skin thoroughly with warm soapy water. Poison ivy rashes sometimes take more than a week to develop. For a short video on identifying poison ivy and tips for prevention, go to fda.gov and search for "outsmarting poison ivy."

## HUNTING SEASON
Hunting is allowed on close to half of Falmouth's conservation lands, and each hike description indicates whether hunting is allowed on that parcel. There are various hunting seasons (deer, pheasant, rabbit, turkey, squirrel) that overlap through the fall and winter. Hunting accidents are extremely rare, but if walking in the woods during hunting season, wearing bright colors or a reflective vest is recommended. Hunting is never allowed on Sunday in Massachusetts. For a complete list of hunting seasons, go to mass.gov and search for "hunting seasons summary." All of mainland Cape Cod falls in Zone 12.

# COLLINS WOODLOT

Molly Johnston

*Collins Woodlot is filled with glacial boulders, some of them covered with large, brown, papery lichens called rock tripe.*

**Length:** 1.2 miles
**Time:** ~30 min

**A network of narrow trails through steeply graded woodland**

## THE HIKE

Collins Woodlot—part of the rolling highlands of the Buzzards Bay Moraine—is one of the most topographically enchanting parcels in Falmouth. Narrow paths wind their way up and down hilly woodland, along a ridgeline, and around a giant glacial depression (to learn how these depressions were formed see the photo caption on page 14). A dense understory of black huckleberry bushes makes for sweet trailside snacking in late summer.

Elizabeth Saito

*Trailing arbutus, the state flower of Massachusetts, is common in Collins Woodlot and throughout Falmouth. The small, fragrant flowers bloom in April before the trees leaf out and shade the ground.*

## THE LAND

Thirty thousand years ago, Cape Cod didn't exist. Instead, the Cape, Martha's Vineyard, Nantucket, and the surrounding seabed was a dry expanse of land more than one hundred miles from the coast. The ocean was 400 feet lower than it is today because so much of the world's water was trapped in a two-mile thick continental glacier that was bearing down on the region at a rate of roughly one foot per day. As the glacier plowed south, it scraped vast amounts of rock up into itself. Around 21,000 years ago, the mass of ice reached its southernmost point, just south of Cape Cod. For the next several thousand years, as the world warmed, the glacier melted at approximately the same rate that it advanced. As it stood in place, huge amounts of rock fell from its melting edge, piling up to form the western and northern ridges of the Cape,

# Collins Woodlot

 Start of suggested route

➤ Suggested route

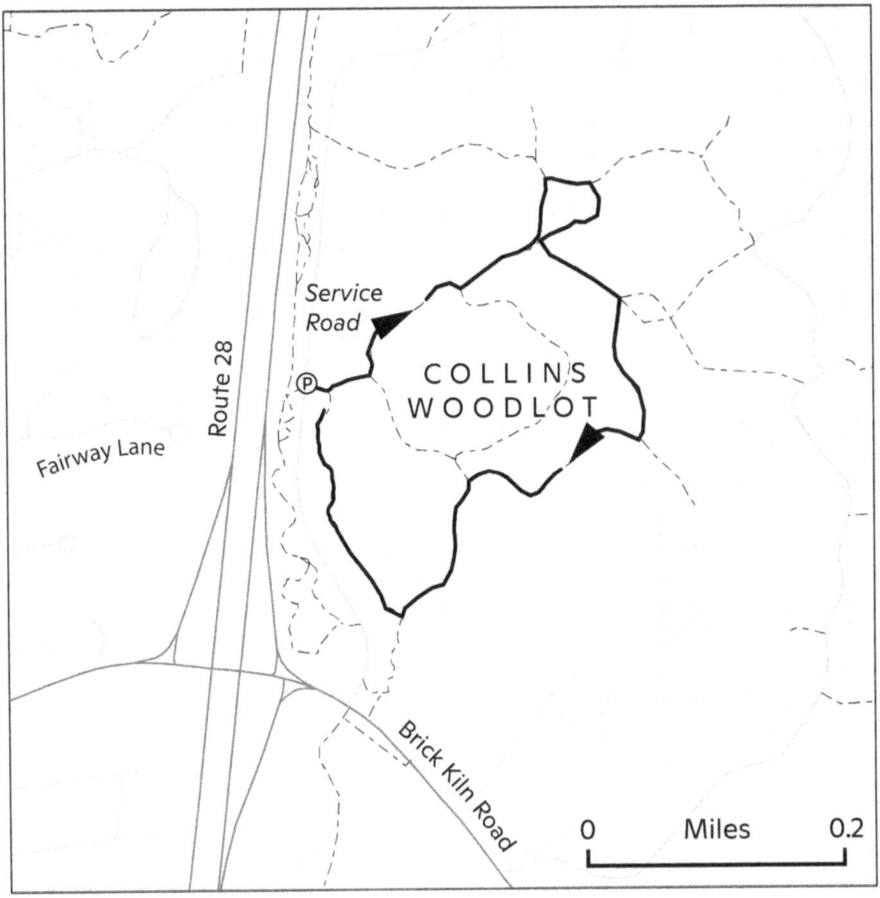

known as the Buzzards Bay and Sandwich Moraines. By 13,000 BC, the glacier had receded past Boston, leaving the Cape high and dry but destined for a watery shoreline.

In the 1920s, a golf course spanned from Collins Woodlot across (the as yet unbuilt) Route 28 and into what is now the Fairway Lane neighborhood in West Falmouth. Plagued by low membership, the course closed in 1938, when, as the *Falmouth Enterprise* wryly noted,

"Engine trouble with the tractor used to mow the fairways, and a spring especially favorable to growing grass, combined to turn the nine fairways into hayfields." When summer resident George Collins (one of the course managers) purchased the southeastern section of the course in 1961, a juvenile pine and oak forest had already sprouted. Twenty-five years later, he sold the land to the town.

## DIRECTIONS AND PARKING

Enter "Service Road" into your navigation app. There is a dirt pullout on the right-hand side of the road a quarter mile north of Service Road's intersection with Brick Kiln Road. The pullout is easy to miss, so keep an eye out for the white and green trailhead sign.

## HUNTING

Hunting is permitted. See page xii for details on hunting seasons.

# THE KNOB

Mark Chester

*The Knob's pinnacle is a popular spot for watching the sunset.*

**Length:** 0.8 miles
**Time:** ~20 min

### A short walk to views of sea and sky

## THE HIKE

A wide trail leads through sheltered coastal thicket to a slender causeway exposed to the elements. Stone steps then lead up to a pinnacle with panoramic views of Buzzards Bay. West across the bay is the Port of New Bedford, the nation's highest grossing fishing port because of its lucrative sea scallop fishery. The city was also the setting for Ishmael's first encounter with the harpooner Queequeg in Herman Melville's *Moby Dick*. Returning from the pinnacle, hikers may wish to take the stairs on the left down to Crescent Beach for a stroll along its curving shoreline. The hike is great for young children.

Mark Chester

*Hikers may wish to explore the small side trails that branch south off The Knob's main trail.*

## THE LAND

This delicate spit of land was willed to the Salt Pond Areas Bird Sanctuaries land trust in 1973 by Cornelia L. Carey, whose family ran a summer hotel on Quissett Harbor for close to a century. The hotel (the large, shingled building with the red trim) is now owned by the Quissett Harbor House Land Trust, while the remainder of the estate was subdivided into the Carey Lane neighborhood to the north. The Knob's 0.8-mile shoreline is a mix of rocky and sandy beach, as well as extensive stone armament that the Quissett Harbor Preservation Trust pays millions of dollars to maintain against the forces of erosion.

For many thousands of years before European settlers sailed to these shores, the Wampanoag people lived on Cape Cod and throughout Southeastern Massachusetts. "Quissett" means "at the place of the small pines." Falmouth—named after the town at the mouth of the river

# The Knob

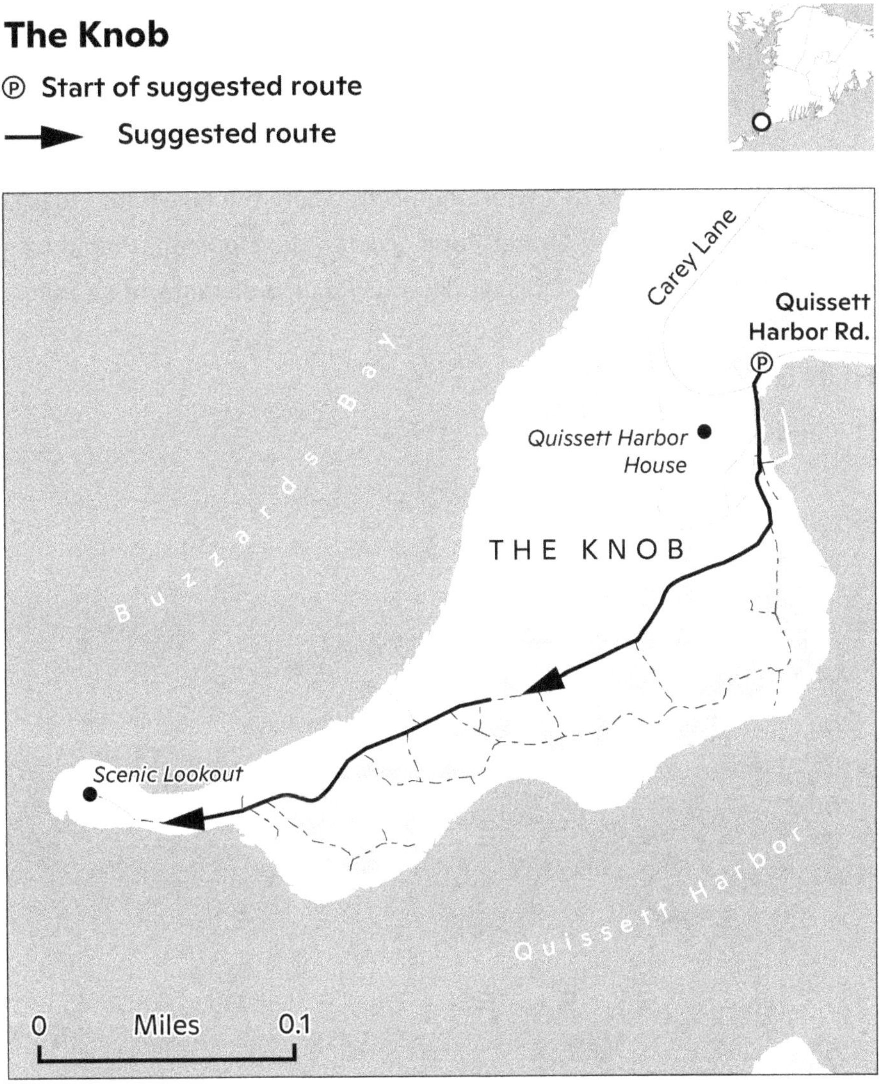

ⓟ Start of suggested route

▶ Suggested route

Fal in England—was incorporated in 1686. On the town seal, underneath the municipality's British name, is a small banner with "Suckanesset," the town's native name, which means "place of the black shells," referring to the shells of quahog clams that were used to make wampum, the traditional currency of the Wampanoag.

## DIRECTIONS AND PARKING

Enter Quissett Harbor into your navigation app. There are two public parking lots on the west side of Quissett Harbor Road, but finding a free space in summer is tantamount to winning the lottery. Cyclists can easily access the property by turning north where the bike path crosses Surf Drive and following Oyster Pond Road to the stoplight, then traveling straight to the end of Quissett Harbor Road, a distance of 1.3 miles.

## HUNTING

Hunting is not allowed.

Mark Chester

# BEEBE WOODS VIA HIGHFIELD DRIVE

Mark Chester

*Many paths in Beebe Woods were created as carriage and bridle trails by the Beebes in the late 1800s. The family's stable was converted into a theater in the 1950s.*

**Length:** 4.2 miles
**Time:** ~1 hr 45 min

**A long woodland walk skirting ponds and pastureland**

## THE HIKE

Beebe Woods, Falmouth's most popular conservation area, hosts a large network of well-worn trails. This route loops through pleasant woodlands, along the banks of two ponds, around a sheep farm, and ends at a historic mansion. The terrain is mostly flat or gently sloped but does feature a steep section that requires scrambling over a few large rocks. The front lawn of Highfield Hall is a nice spot to spread a picnic blanket.

Tom Noonan

*The Beebes purchased Ice House Pond for the sole purpose of supplying the family with ice during the summer. Huge blocks cut from the frozen pond and insulated with straw had enough thermal mass to last a year.*

## THE LAND

Located just west of downtown Falmouth, Beebe Woods was originally the 700-acre summer estate of the Beebe family of Boston, who'd amassed a fortune through trade in the mid-nineteenth century. After the last of the Beebe children died without an heir in 1932, the property changed hands many times. Various visions for the estate—sanatorium, religious retreat, research laboratory—never came to fruition. In the 1960s, a 500-unit residential development seemed poised to succeed, but the town threw up a series of permitting roadblocks, hoping to save the property from subdivision. Just weeks before the sale was set to go through, local philanthropists Josephine and Josiah K. Lilly III bought the entire property and donated 388 acres to the townspeople of Falmouth.

In 1992, the dilapidated family mansion, Highfield Hall, was slated for demolition, but a decade of lobbying by historic preservationists

# Beebe Woods via. Highfield Drive

 Start of suggested route

➤ Suggested route

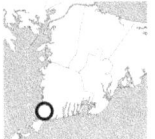

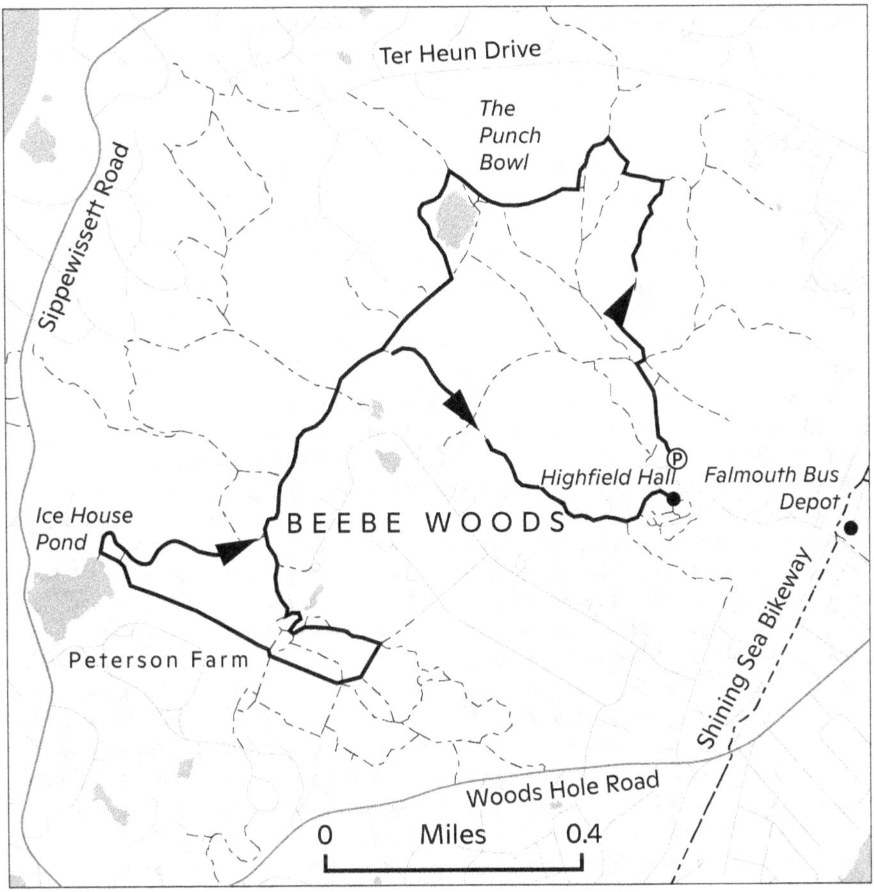

staved off the wrecking ball. An $8.5 million renovation—funded entirely by private donations and volunteer labor from local contractors—restored the Queen Anne–style mansion to its former glory. Owned by the town but operated by a nonprofit, Highfield Hall now hosts art exhibits, music concerts, and cooking classes and is rented out for weddings. The rundown ice house on the property was restored in 2006 and is one of the few remaining ice houses on the Cape.

## DIRECTIONS AND PARKING

Enter "56 Highfield Drive" into your phone or GPS. Pass Highfield Hall on your left. Continue along the one-way road as it curves to the right. A large parking lot with a trail kiosk will be on your left. To access Beebe Woods from the bike path, turn west at the Falmouth Bus Depot and follow the road all the way to the top of the hill.

## HUNTING

Hunting is not allowed.

Elizabeth Saito

# BEEBE WOODS via KELLY WOODLAND

Dorene Sykes

*In wintertime, Buzzards Bay is visible through the bare trees at the top of this hill, which rises 140 feet above sea level, the highest elevation in Beebe Woods.*

**Length:** 2.4 miles
**Time:** ~1 hr

**A looped hike through hilly woodland, circling a glacial pond**

## THE HIKE

This hike takes you through a second-growth forest of oaks, pines, and beeches. Dense thickets of huckleberry flank meandering paths criss-crossed by lichen-covered stone walls. The hike circles a small glacial pond with a tiny sandy beach on its northeast shore. On the return trip, the path appears to terminate at a private residence off Haynes Avenue but actually continues along the border of the property for a short way before turning back into the woods.

Mark Chester

*The Punch Bowl is a kettle-hole pond, which began as a depression formed at the end of the last ice age when the retreating glacier left behind large chunks of ice buried in sediment. The chunks eventually melted, leaving behind scalloped bowls of earth, many of which later filled with groundwater.*

## THE LAND

When Henry David Thoreau visited Cape Cod in the mid-1800s, he dubbed it the "bare and bended arm of Massachusetts." The Cape Cod Thoreau encountered was a windswept expanse of farm and pasture land. But through the twentieth century—as tourism replaced agriculture as the Cape's dominant industry—trees repopulated the peninsula. Beebe Woods tells this history in microcosm. In the mid-1800s, when the Beebe family of Boston bought 700 acres of hilly land near the tiny village of Falmouth for their summer estate, Beebe "Woods" was actually a patchwork of pastures enclosed by hand-built stone walls. The Beebes then planted trees and encouraged the natural regrowth of the forest. Though the property is now entirely wooded, stone walls snaking through the forest are telltales of the land's agricultural past.

# Beebe Woods via. Kelly Woodland

ⓟ Start of suggested route

➤ Suggested route

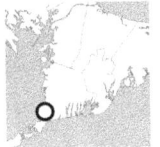

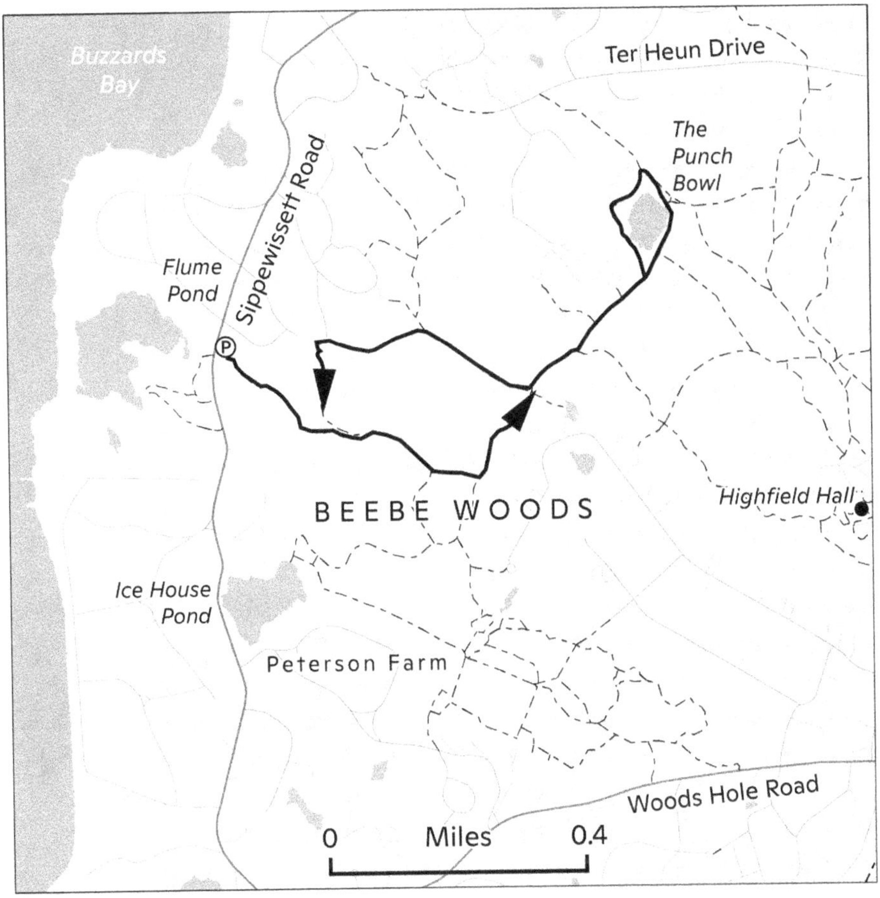

In 1972, when Falmouth still had large tracts of undeveloped juvenile forest but few conservation parcels, local benefactors Josiah and Josephine Lilly bought the Beebe property and gifted nearly 400 acres to the town. Forty years later, The 300 Committee Land Trust and the Buzzards Bay Coalition bought the three-acre Kelly parcel along Sippewissett Road, enabling public access to Beebe Woods through its western slopes. Across the street is the Flume Pond conservation area, which contains freshwater wetlands, vernal pools, a saltwater pond, and ocean shoreline. Together, these three parcels create a wildlife corridor where diverse species—terrestrial, aerial and aquatic—can find shelter, food, and breeding grounds. Beebe Woods' mammalian inhabitants include deer, foxes, raccoons, skunks, rabbits, coyotes, and fishers.

## DIRECTIONS AND PARKING

Enter "Kelly Woodland" into your navigation app. There is a clearly marked dirt parking lot on the eastern side of Sippewissett Road between numbers 298 and 318.

## HUNTING

Hunting is not allowed.

# COONAMESSETT RIVER

Elizabeth Saito

*Diverse plants are returning to the banks of the Coonamessett River after decades of monoculture cranberry farming.*

**Length:** 3 miles
**Time:** ~1 hr 15 min

**A pondside trail and long loop around former cranberry bogs**

## THE HIKE

This hike takes you along the wooded shoreline of a small pond and then in a long loop around the wetland meadows of the Coonamessett River. The hike is loveliest in fall when goldenrod, purple aster, and other autumn wildflowers are in bloom. The trail around the river is wide, sandy, and flat, but the narrow pondside trail has a few steep sections. The entire lower third of the riverside trail (including the boardwalks over Swift and Dexter's Crossings) is handicapped accessible as well as the first tenth of a mile of the northern trail that runs alongside Pond 14.

Elizabeth Saito

*A fish ladder between Pond 14 and the Coonamessett River aids herring and eels migrating between the Atlantic and Coonamessett Pond.*

## THE LAND

The history of human relations with the Coonamessett River has four major epochs. The first is subsistence fishing. For thousands of years, the Wampanoag peoples harvested abundant herring and eels from the Coonamessett, which means "place of the long fish." In 1700, colonists dammed the river to power a mill that ground grain into flour and sawed timber into planks; the building was later converted into a wool processing factory that produced a sturdy cloth popular with Falmouth fishermen and whalers. In 1890, the wetlands around the river were converted into cranberry bogs. "Cranberry" is derived from the Pilgrim name for the plant, "craneberry," so-called because the fruit's springtime flower, with its long downward-pointing bundle of stamens, resembles the head and bill of a crane. Cranberry production exploded on Cape Cod in the late

# Coonamessett River

ⓟ Start of suggested route

▶ Suggested route

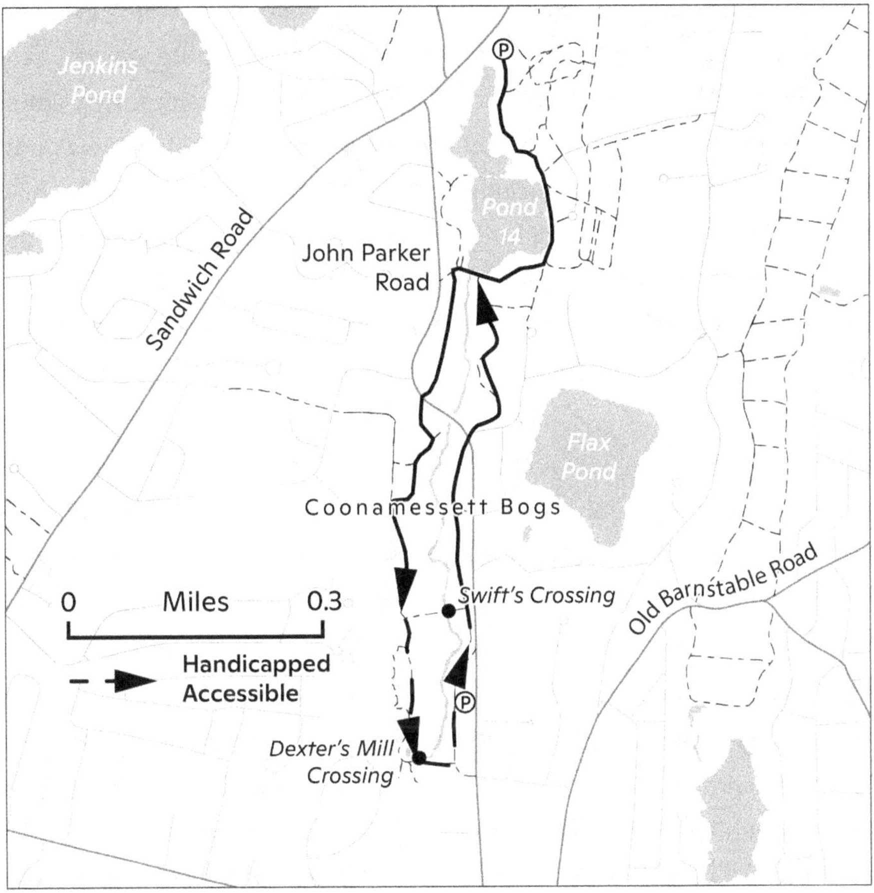

Handicapped Accessible

nineteenth century: the acreage under cultivation in Falmouth jumped from twenty-six to 343 acres in twenty years. One hundred years later, the current epoch was ushered in: environmental restoration.

Cranberry growers routinely spread sand on their bogs. This creates a well-drained soil ideal for cranberries but suppresses the growth of other plants. In 2018, conservationists excavated several feet of sand from atop the bogs to expose the underlying peat. In short order, seeds of native wetland plants that had lain dormant in the peat for over a century sprouted up in abundance. The sand had also accumulated in the river, making it wide, shallow, and warm. Because river herring do best in a deep, narrow river—where they can hide from predators—removing the sand helps these migratory fish reach their spring spawning grounds in Coonamessett Pond. The river had also been straightened for cranberry farming, which makes flooding and draining the bogs easier. When the bogs were restored to wetland meadow, a sinuous channel was dug for the Coonamessett, mimicking its former bends and curves. The new channel, which is 30 percent longer, is anchored with giant, upright logs. A deep, winding river is cooler and more hospitable to trout and eels.

## DIRECTIONS AND PARKING

Enter "Bartolomei Conservation Area" into your navigation app. The turnoff to the parking lot is on the east side of Sandwich Road, just north of the junction with John Parker Road. The entrance to the lower river is at 100 John Parker Road. The John Parker lot features a wheelchair-accessible overlook that provides an aerial view of the river valley.

## HUNTING

Hunting is not allowed on the lower riverside portion of the hike. However, winter duck hunting is permitted along the upper Pond 14 section of the hike. See page xii for details on hunting seasons.

# HEADWATERS OF OYSTER POND

Elizabeth Saito

*Vernal pools—seasonal wetlands—are home to the much beloved "spring peeper" frog.*

**Length:** 0.7 miles
**Time:** ~25 min

### A trek through coastal woodland abutting a public garden

## THE HIKE

The small size of this parcel belies its topographical and ecological diversity. Vernal pools, sloping groves of beech trees, a ridgeline, a small creek, and an enormous natural amphitheater present themselves to the nature enthusiast like scenes in a fast-paced drama. Its tight grouping of crisscrossing trails makes it an ideal hike for children, who can choose to go this way or that without getting too far afield. The suggested route follows the trails blazed in blue. Spohr Gardens, a public garden with views across Oyster Pond, abuts the property and is a lovely spot for a picnic.

Tom Noonan

*The ample shade and dense root structures of beech trees crowd out groundling competitors, allowing for a unique depth of vision through the forest. (However, the foremost trunk in this photo is that of a pitch pine, recognizable by its dark, scaly bark. Beech tree bark is smooth and gray.)*

## THE LAND

This parcel contains two vernal pools, a critically endangered habitat in Massachusetts. These ephemeral pools swell with water in the spring and then dry out in summer, making them uninhabitable for fish. Absent these predators, amphibians prosper. In spring, gelatinous blobs of frog and salamander eggs lie thick on the surface of the pools. Frogs and salamanders begin life as gill-breathing aquatic creatures, then morph into lung-breathing land dwellers. "Amphibian" is derived from the ancient Greek word *amphibious*, which means "to live a double life," a compound of *amphi* (of both kinds) and *bios* (life). In spring, tiny frogs known as "peepers" belt out a thunderous choral thrill at sundown and all through the night from their vernal pool breeding grounds.

# Headwaters of Oyster Pond

 Start of suggested route
➤ Suggested route

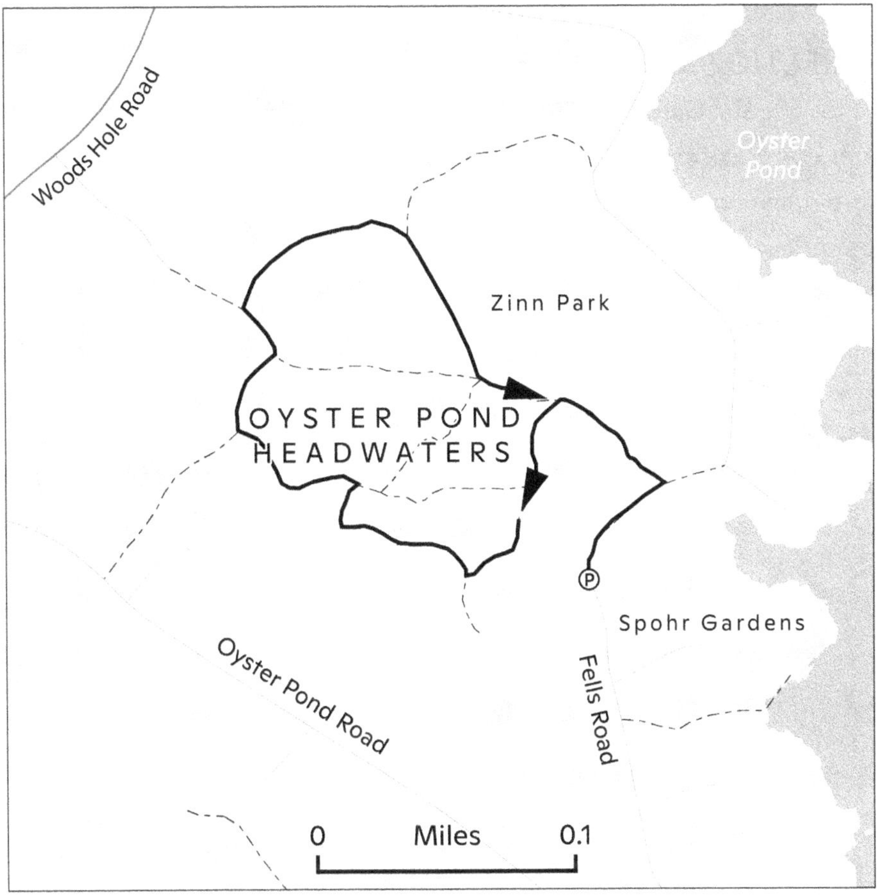

In the 1990s, scientist Dr. Holger Jannasch donated twenty-two of the property's twenty-nine acres to the Woods Hole Oceanographic Institution (WHOI). Twenty years later, WHOI sold the land for $2 million to the Oyster Pond Environmental Trust, which already owned the neighboring seven-acre Zinn Park. A housing development proposed for Zinn Park in the mid-1980s spurred local conservationists to purchase the land to protect the pond's water quality. Forests and wetlands act as natural sponges, soaking nitrogen from septic systems up out of the groundwater before it reaches the pond. Every plant on the property also breathes in carbon dioxide, drawing the greenhouse gas out of the atmosphere and converting its carbon molecules into trunks, branches, twigs, and leaves.

## DIRECTIONS AND PARKING

Enter "Spohr Gardens" into your navigation app. A small parking area and trail kiosk are beyond the garden at the end of Fells Road. To access by bicycle, turn west off the bike path onto Surf Drive, take the first right onto Oyster Pond Road, and then go right at the next fork onto Fells Road.

## HUNTING

Hunting is not allowed.

# LONG POND & GOODWILL PARK

Mark Chester

*One mile long and sixty-five feet deep, Long Pond supplies most of the town's drinking water. Falmouth is the only town on the Cape to draw its drinking water from a pond; all other municipalities rely on wells drilled into the aquifer.*

**Length:** 4.1 miles (7.5 miles)
**Time:** ~1 hr 20 min (~2 hr 45 min)

**A hike through forest encircling Falmouth's reservoir**

## THE HIKE

This hike takes you along the rising and falling shoreline of Long Pond, Falmouth's drinking water reservoir. Towering white pines flank the wide and well-traveled paths. Hikers will pass along a slender isthmus between Long Pond and Grews Pond where the town's original water pumping station stands. Swimming is prohibited in Long Pond but is allowed at neighboring Grews Pond in Goodwill Park. Dozens of picnic tables with standing metal BBQ grills are located under the trees surrounding the park's playground.

Milt Williamson

*The steam engines and machinery of the early pumping station required the around-the-clock attention of a full-time engineer who lived with his wife in a nine-foot-wide dwelling space partitioned off from the pump room with wood planking. In 1904, a stone and brick apartment (left) was added on for the couple.*

## HIKE EXTENSION

For a longer hike, include a visit to Collins Woodlot (see map on page 3) by taking the spur at the northwestern tip of the pond and keeping left until you hit Brick Kiln Road. Cross Brick Kiln and proceed up Service Road a short distance until you see a path back into the forest on your right.

## THE LAND

Falmouth residents began drawing drinking water from Long Pond in 1898. Over the following decades, the town acquired the surrounding land, totaling 585 acres, to protect the health of the pond. The southern seventy acres comprising Goodwill Park were donated in 1894 by Joseph Story Fay. Fay amassed a fortune shipping cotton to New England mills and became one of Falmouth's first summer residents when, in

# Long Pond

ⓟ Start of suggested route

➤ Suggested route

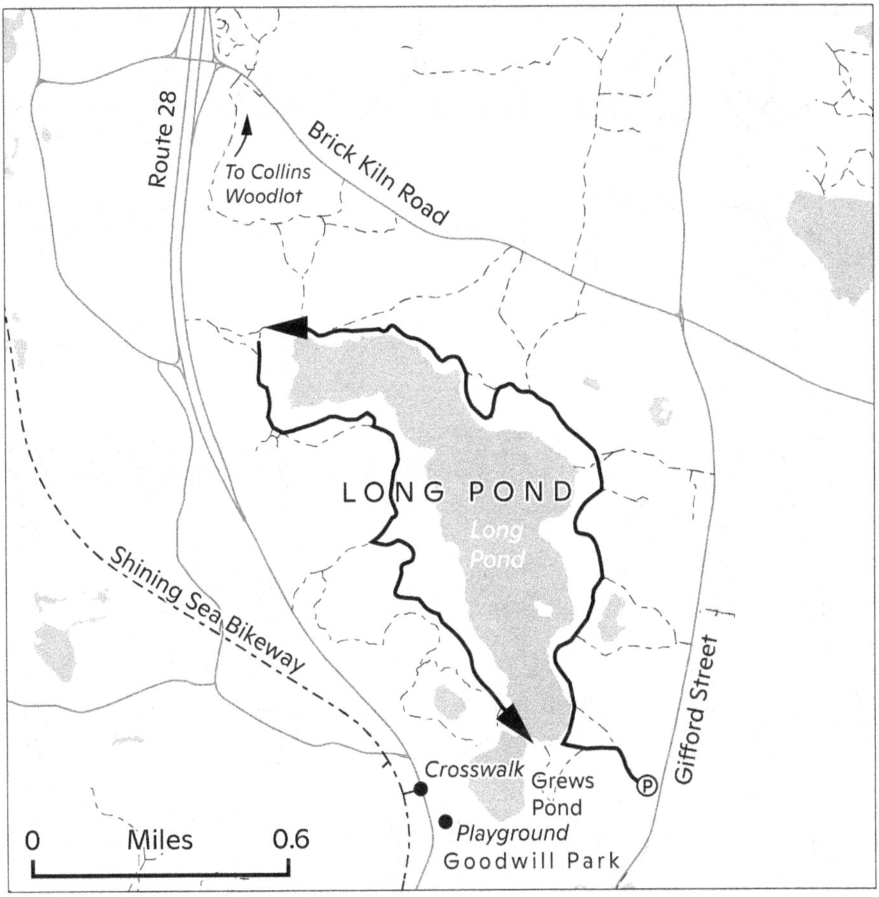

1850, he bought an estate overlooking Little Harbor in Woods Hole. An enthusiastic horticulturist, Fay then bought hundreds of acres throughout town and began planting trees on the overgrazed land. When he donated Goodwill Park to the town, Fay stipulated that alcohol, gambling, and horse racing were prohibited in perpetuity and that the land must remain "a pleasure park free to all well-conducted persons." Thus, Goodwill Park's Grews Pond is the only municipal beach where parking is free year-round.

When the original Long Pond pumping station was built in 1898, Falmouth had seven public hand-pump wells, located at village intersections and schoolhouses. Fires were fought by bucket brigades from the nearest water source. Two summer residents organized private investors to finance construction of a pump house and sixteen miles of cast-iron water mains connecting to ninety-seven fire hydrants. Then, four years later, they sold the company to the town for $158,291. In 2014, Falmouth voters agreed to replace the aged system with a $45-million water filtration plant built on the Long Pond's eastern shore. The old pump station, which is listed on the National Register of Historic Places, is currently used to house town documents.

## DIRECTIONS AND PARKING

Park in the dirt lot just inside the Gifford Street entrance to Goodwill Park. A short drive farther into the park leads to Grews Pond and then a playground. Parking at Goodwill Park fills up quickly in the summer. To access the park via the Shining Sea Bikeway, take the paved spur just north of 620 Palmer Avenue (Route 28) to a crosswalk leading to the park's pedestrian entrance. The park cannot be accessed by car off Route 28; the entrances are gated shut.

## HUNTING

Hunting is permitted. See page xii for details on hunting seasons.

# QUASHNET RIVER

Dorene Sykes

*When the Quashnet River crosses south under Route 28, it gets a new name, the Moonakis River, and then empties into Waquoit Bay.*

**Length:** 2.8 miles
**Time:** ~1 hr 10 min

### A hike along the wooded banks of a quiet river

## THE HIKE

This hike runs north through pretty woodlands along the western bank of the Quashnet River, crosses the river, and then returns south along the eastern bank. The western shore is sunny and open, with oak as the dominant tree species; the eastern shore, where pines dominate, is dark and moist. Several spurs off the main path lead down to the riverbank, affording glimpses of this clean, swift river.

Dorene Sykes

*In colonial times, the strong, straight trunks of white pines were prized as ship masts. In 1691, the relatively treeless England claimed all white pines in Massachusetts over two feet in diameter as property of the British Crown, angering colonists who had to get permission and pay fees to cut them down.*

## THE LAND

The Quashnet River has a long history of human use. Originally, the river and its surrounding lands were fished and hunted by the Wampanoag peoples, who have lived in Southeastern Massachusetts for over 12,000 years and were the first Native Americans to greet the Pilgrims. Early European settlers cleared the river's shore for pasture. At the turn of the nineteenth century, the Quashnet—prized for its abundant brook trout—was dammed for a mill, preventing fish from migrating upstream to their spring spawning grounds. Then, in the 1890s, the land around the river was leveled and converted into cranberry bogs. Each year, sand, pesticides and fertilizers were dumped on the bogs, and fish populations further dwindled. In 1954, after Hurricane Carol flooded the bogs

# Quashnet River

Ⓟ Start of suggested route
➡ Suggested route

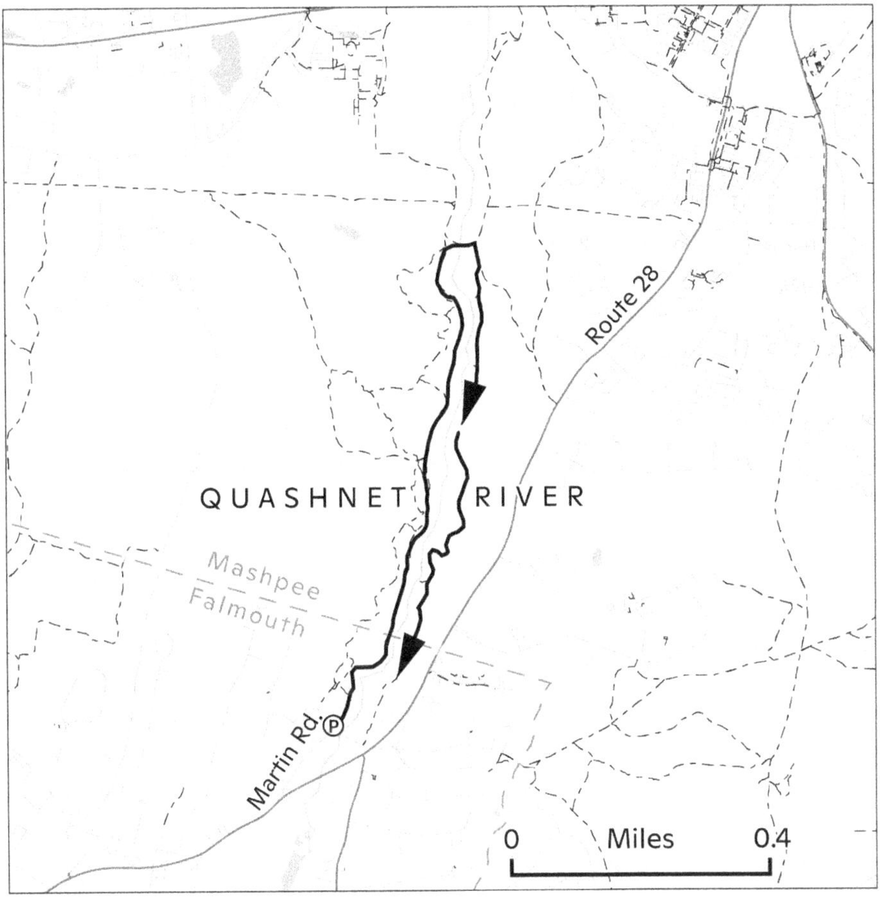

with saltwater and damaged their infrastructure, cranberry farming was abandoned.

In 1986, the Quashnet Coalition—a consortium of conservationists, Wampanoag tribe members, and nonprofits—was formed to block the development of a 580-unit condominium complex proposed for the Quashnet River Valley. The state chipped in $10 million to purchase 336 acres along the river, which is now part of the 6,000-acre Mashpee

National Wildlife Refuge. The nonprofit Trout Unlimited spearheaded an ecological restoration of the river, which had grown shallow, sluggish, warm, and otherwise inhospitable to brook trout that thrive in deep, cool waters. The swift, slender river seen today, shaded with native shrubs along its banks, now hosts abundant fish and wildlife.

## DIRECTIONS & PARKING

Enter "Martin Road" into your navigation app. The road is off Route 28, just before the Mashpee town line. A clearly marked dirt parking lot lies west of where Martin Road bridges the river.

## HUNTING

Hunting is permitted. See page xii for details on hunting seasons.

# BOURNE FARM & WING POND WOODS

Mark Chester

*Bourne Farm was a working farm for nearly three centuries. Today, income is generated by renting the bucolic property for weddings and other events.*

**Length:** 1.6 miles
**Time:** ~40 min

**A walk through fields, woodlands, and around a cranberry bog**

## THE HIKE

This hike begins in fields surrounding a historic farmhouse, passes underneath the bike path via a stone tunnel (originally used to herd cattle under the railroad tracks), crosses two woodland streams, and circles a cranberry bog. Hikers must possess a certain level of agility because crossing the second stream requires balancing atop two narrow concrete slabs or taking a flying leap to the opposite bank. The less sure-footed can walk to the herring run, backtrack, and then view the cranberry bogs by walking north along the bike path. The mowed hillside overlooking Crockers Pond is a great picnic spot.

Elizabeth Saito

*In spring, herring swim upstream through the marshes west of Old Silver Beach and along this creek to spawn in the fresh waters of Wing Pond.*

## THE LAND

Deeds for the Bourne Farm property date to 1678, eight years before Falmouth's incorporation as a town. Selectman David Crowell purchased the property in 1774 and built the farmhouse the following year. Over the next 200 years, the farm passed to a nonfamily member only once when the childless grandson of David Crowell left the property to a faithful farmhand, Justus Davis. John Avery (who married Justus Davis's granddaughter) left the farm to his grandson, Lester Bourne Sr., who had cared for him in his old age. In 1979, Lester Jr. and Eulinda Bourne—of Eulinda's Ice Cream in West Falmouth—sold the land to the Salt Pond Areas Bird Sanctuaries land trust, which enrolled the farm on the National Register of Historic Places.

In 1986, Falmouth residents voted to purchase the nineteen-acre

# Bourne Farm and Wing Pond Woods

 Start of suggested route

➡ Suggested route

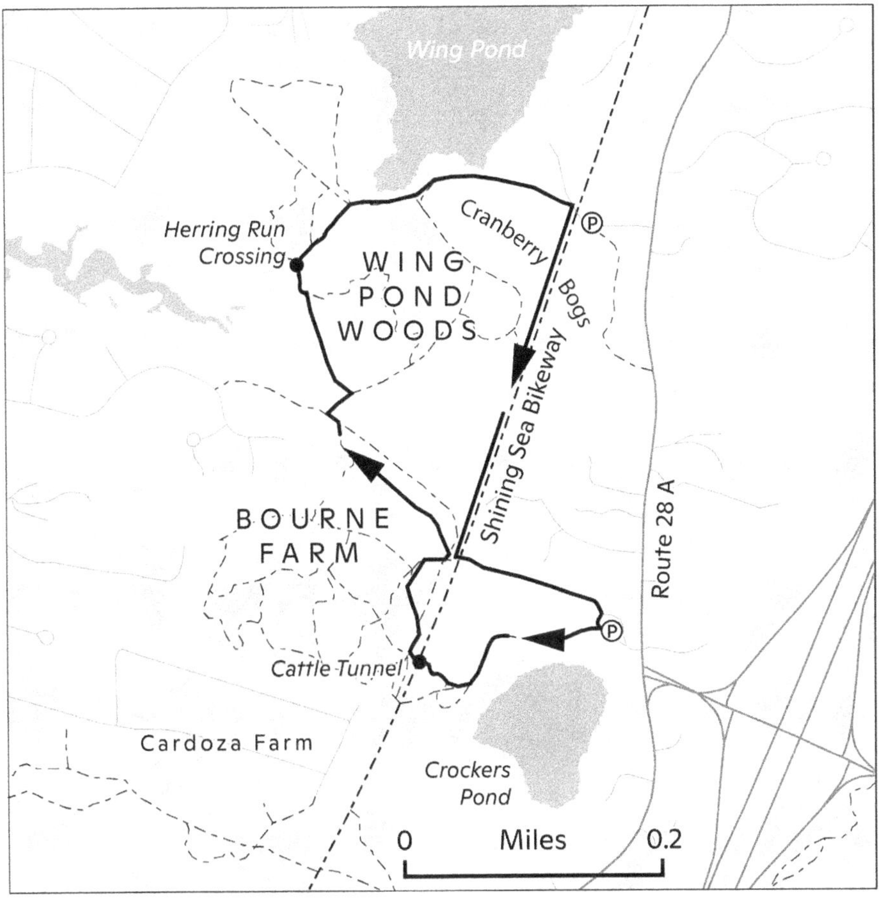

Wing Pond Woods parcel that borders Bourne Farm to the north. The sale was brokered by The 300 Committee, a land trust established with the goal of preserving 300 acres of land to celebrate the town's 300th anniversary. (The group went on to preserve over 2,500 acres of open space in Falmouth.) The private cranberry bogs abutting the property have been in operation since at least the 1950s and are flooded at harvest time with water from Wing Pond.

## DIRECTIONS AND PARKING

Enter "Bourne" Farm into your navigation app. The entrance to the farm is just across from Thomas Landers Road's junction with Route 28A. Parking is for Bourne Farm visitors only and not as access to the bike path. The nearest public parking lot for the bike path is 1.5 miles south of the farm at the bike path's intersection with Old Dock Road. Bourne Farm is frequently closed to the public during private functions throughout the summer. Public access to the contiguous Wing Pond Woods parcel is from a dirt drive on the west side of Route 28A just north of the cranberry bogs.

## HUNTING

Hunting is not allowed at Bourne Farm.

Mark Chester

## TEATICKET PARK

Mark Chester

*Handicapped-accessible trails of crushed stone curve through Teaticket Park's grasslands.*

**Length:** 0.4 miles
**Time:** ~10 min

**A wetland meadow in the heart of a busy neighborhood**

## THE HIKE

The restored meadow in the heart of this modest little park provides a welcome sense of wildness amidst the heavily developed Route 28 corridor in Teaticket. A scenic trail—portions of which are handicapped accessible—loops through swaths of tall grasses, a patch of woodland, and around a small marsh. The short loop is well suited for small children.

Mark Chester

*Teaticket Park's tiny creek flows south around the back of the Falmouth Mall and into Little Pond. Old-timers in town remember skating on bogs that were later filled in to build the mall and its parking lot.*

## THE LAND

For sixty years, patrons of Joe's Driving Range sent their balls flying across the eleven-acre sweep of land now known as Teaticket Park. That era came to an end when, in 2011, The 300 Committee Land Trust bought the property and gave it an ecological makeover. Once mowers no longer rumbled over the tidily maintained turf, wild grasses began to regrow; the wetland stopped absorbing chemical fertilizers, and its edges were planted with native shrubs; rich soil was spread along the upper streetscape; and a small army of volunteers nursed and watered sixty-eight saplings and two acres of newly planted grass through the hot summer months. Hundreds of golf balls were removed from the property and are still being found today.

In 2014, after the park's natural complexion had been coaxed back to the fore, active restoration ceased, and the wetland meadow and sandplain

# Teaticket Park

Ⓟ  Start of suggested route

➤  Suggested route

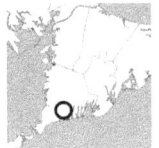

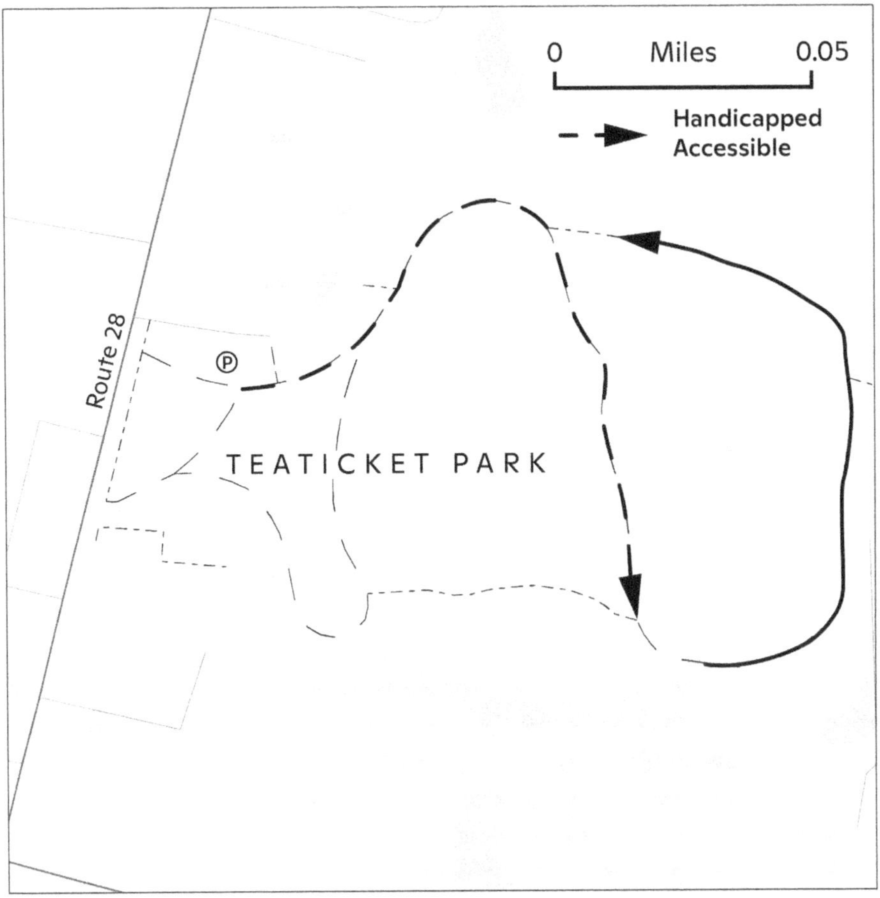

grassland portions of the park were left to their own ecological devices. Huge, cushiony mats of ground moss have since colonized the moist land around the low-lying marsh, and most of the park's saplings survived to young adulthood. Many birds call the park's trees home, including Song Sparrows, Black-capped Chickadees, and Downy Woodpeckers. Killdeer, shorebirds in the plover family that nest on the ground, can be spotted skittering about as they hunt for grasshoppers and beetles.

## DIRECTIONS AND PARKING

Enter "Teaticket Park" (205 Teaticket Highway) into your navigation app. The parking lot is on the west side of Route 28, across the street from Cumberland Farms and Figuerido Way.

## HUNTING

Hunting is not allowed.

# SHALLOW POND WOODLANDS & BREIVOGEL PONDS

Dorene Sykes

*The two ponds on the Breivogel land were originally dug to provide water to grow beach grass, which owner Carl Breivogel sold to nurseries and municipalities. Mr. Breivogel stocked the ponds with bass and invited young anglers to fish.*

**Length:** 2.7 miles
**Time:** ~1 hr 5 min

### A hike through woodlands and sandplain grassland

## THE HIKE

The ecological diversity of this hike makes it one of the most enjoyable in town. A dense, needle-coated woodland of pitch pines and young white pines gives way to open understory beneath towering, mature white pines. The route next threads between two man-made ponds edged with cattails. Hikers then trek through a wide sandplain grassland and circle restored vernal pools before heading back into the forest.

Dorene Sykes

*In spring, thousands of toad and frog eggs can be seen floating on the surface of restored vernal pools. Amphibians, which rely on vernal pools to breed, are going extinct at a fast rate because of climate change and habitat loss.*

## THE LAND

Two parcels link to form this 138-acre tract of protected open space. The western half was formerly a gravel and sand mining pit owned by Carl Breivogel. The land was approved for a thirty-two–unit subdivision, but Mr. Breivogel instead sold it to the town in 2003 at a bargain price. Mr. Breivogel proposed and then contributed to an ecological restoration fund used to plant native grasses on fifteen sandy acres and dig a series of vernal pools (seasonal wetlands that dry out in summer). In 2017, when The 300 Committee Land Trust paid $1.4 million for the adjacent seventy acres of woodland around Shallow Pond, the parcel was the largest remaining tract of undeveloped privately owned land in Falmouth.

Roughly 16,000 years ago, at the end of the last ice age, when the huge glacier that plowed up the ridged spine of the Upper Cape melted,

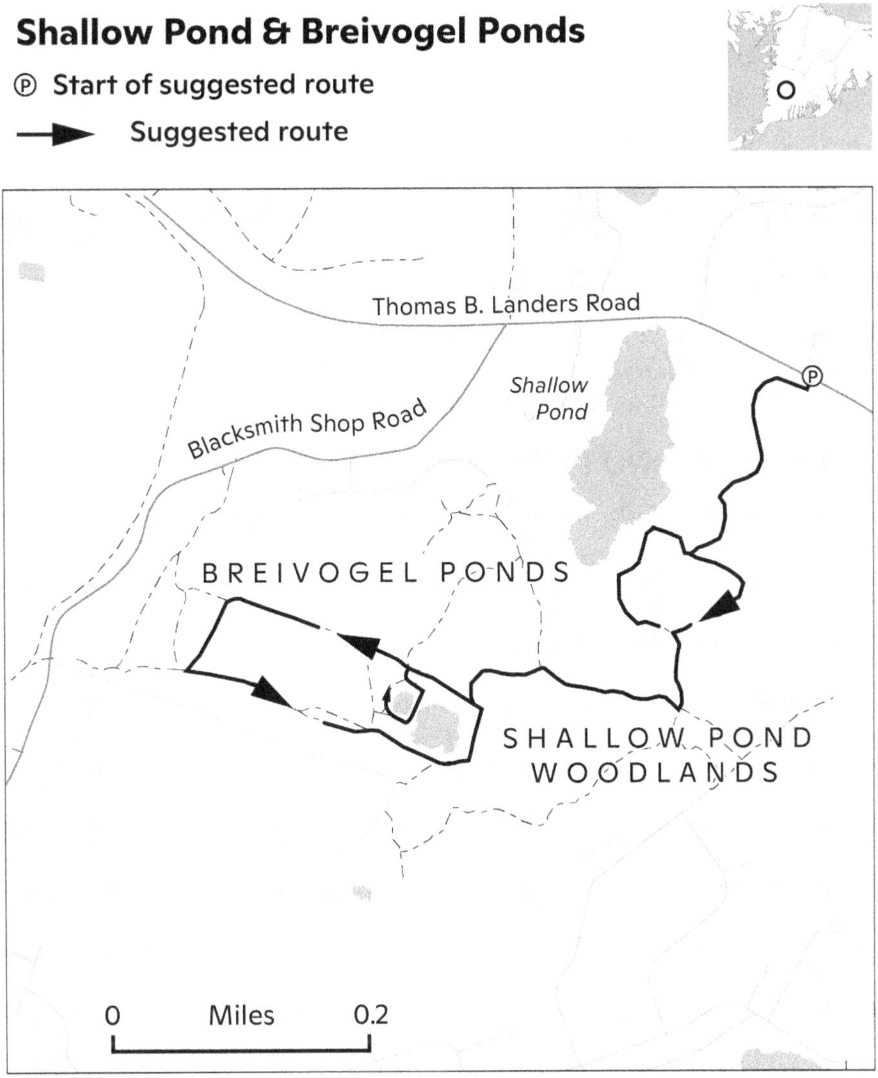

# Shallow Pond & Breivogel Ponds

ⓟ Start of suggested route

▶ Suggested route

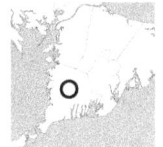

the Cape was a barren expanse of sand and gravel. Pioneer plants then began to colonize the nutrient-poor soil. Over thousands of years, enough topsoil accumulated for forests to find a footing above the barren plain. When the Breivogel property became a gravel mine, that process was reversed: the forest and topsoil were scraped away to expose the underlying sand. A sandplain grassland is a globally rare habitat that must be managed closely to prevent it from reverting to forest. Every year, volunteers handpick hundreds of baby pitch pines out of the sandy soil. Once the grasses become firmly established, the plain can be mowed or burned to prevent forests from taking hold. Dirt bikes and four-wheelers are prohibited, but nonetheless, they frequently zoom over the parcel, squashing grasses and eroding the soil. Sandplain grasslands provide mouse hunting territory for hawks and owls and nesting and feeding grounds for many smaller birds, including the Grasshopper Sparrow; close to a dozen butterflies classified as species of "conservation concern" are dependent on sandplain grasslands.

## DIRECTIONS AND PARKING

Enter "Shallow Ponds Woodlands" into your navigation app. A clearly marked parking lot is on the south side of Thomas Landers Road, just west of 225 Thomas Landers Road.

## HUNTING

Hunting is permitted. See page xii for details on hunting seasons.

# SEA FARMS MARSH

Elizabeth Saito

*Black Duck Cove is home to great blue herons, ospreys, marsh hawks, and a variety of ducks.*

**Length:** 1.3 miles
**Time:** ~30 min

**A woodland walk with views of a salt marsh and coastal pond**

## THE HIKE

Amidst the heavily developed Davisville neighborhood, entering Sea Farms Marsh feels like slipping into a secret world. This secluded peninsula is flanked on both sides by Bournes Pond, a coastal saltwater pond. A spur at the beginning of the hike leads down to a bench with views of Black Duck Cove. The trail culminates on a thin strip of beach along Bournes Pond and then loops back along a parallel track to the parking lot. The terrain is flat, making it a good choice for less sure-footed hikers.

Elizabeth Saito

*Saltwater marshes help protect coastal communities by buffering them against storms and flooding.*

## THE LAND

The Davisville neighborhood was open farmland through the first half of the twentieth century, but Sea Farms Marsh conservation area actually got its name from a short-lived aquaculture research station, Sea Farm Research Foundation, established on an old chicken farm in the 1960s. The land was then purchased by the town in three chunks: forty-six acres in 1985, followed by two twenty-acre plots in 1988 and 1998.

When the Cape's economy shifted sharply towards tourism after the Second World War, much of the farmland occupying the narrow strips of land between Falmouth's eastern coastal ponds was sold to developers. Today, the ponds suffer from eutrophication, an overabundance of the nutrient nitrogen, which causes algae to grow rampant, choking out

# Sea Farms Marsh

Ⓟ Start of suggested route

▶ Suggested route

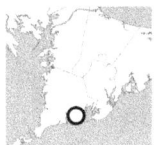

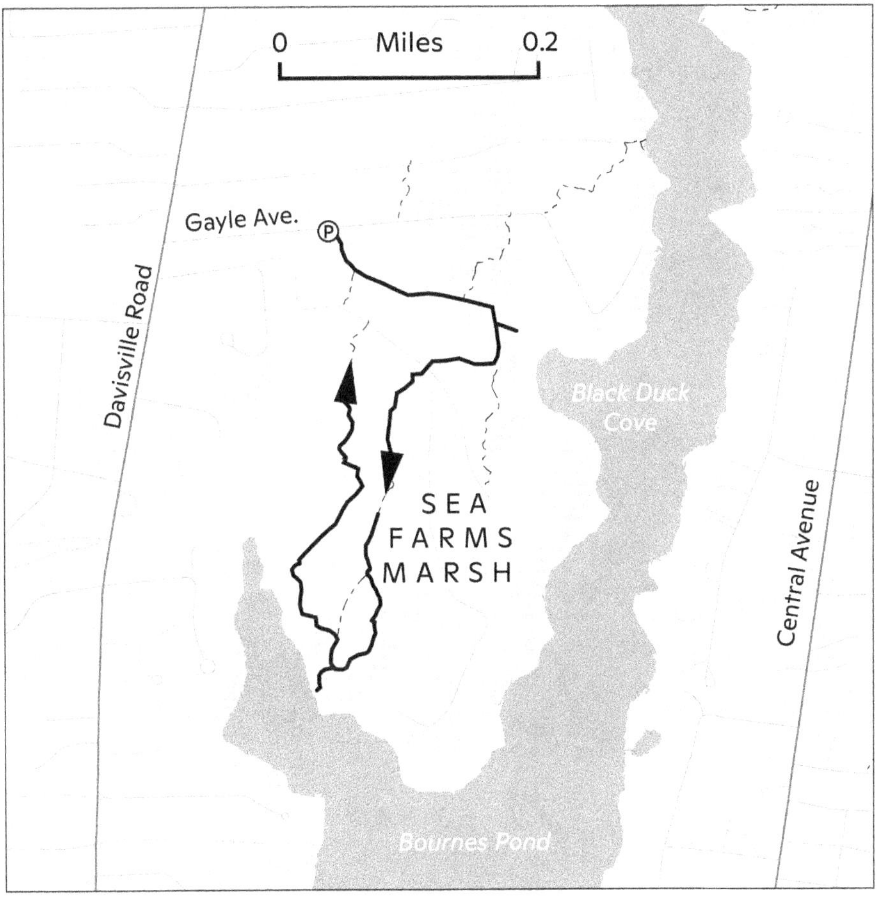

fish and eelgrass. Nitrogen (a major component of urine) leaches into groundwater via septic systems and then flows into the bays. Falmouth is in the midst of a decades-long effort to clean up its estuaries by sewering densely populated neighborhoods. Marshes and forests act as natural sponges for nitrogen, harmlessly soaking up the nutrient before it reaches the bays.

## DIRECTIONS AND PARKING

Enter "Gayle Road" into your navigation app. A small dirt parking area is on the right, shortly after the paved section of Gayle Road ends.

## HUNTING

Hunting is not allowed.

# ASHUMET HOLLY WILDLIFE SANCTUARY

Elizabeth Saito

*The Ashumet Holly Reservation contains over sixty-five varieties of holly trees and is a lovely parcel to snowshoe around after a winter storm.*

**Length:** 0.6 miles
**Time:** ~15 min

**A stroll through holly-studded woodland with pond views**

## THE HIKE

This short amble through fields, woodland, and along the bank of a coastal plain pond is a great hike for small children. The gentle ups and downs, twisting paths, and views across the pond make for a pleasantly varied walk. The hike can be easily extended by circling the entire pond.

Dorene Sykes

*Grassy Pond, a coastal plain pond, is resplendent with rare pond-shore wildflowers in the summer and fall and attracts over thirty species of dragonflies.*

## THE LAND

The forty-five–acre Ashumet Holly Wildlife Sanctuary, now owned by the Massachusetts Audubon Society, was once part of a large farm purchased in 1924 by Wilfrid Wheeler, the state's Commissioner of Agriculture. Distressed by the decline of the Cape's native hollies due to overharvesting, Wheeler dedicated part of his farm as a holly nursery, selling juvenile plants for home landscaping. Wheeler's collection of native and exotic hollies drew large crowds in December, when visitors could purchase sustainably harvested holiday cuttings and admire the bright red berries amid the winter landscape.

Wilfrid Wheeler died on Christmas Day 1961. The holly acreage of Ashumet Farm was then purchased by Falmouth philanthropist Josiah K. Lilly III, the great grandson of the founder of the Lilly pharmaceutical

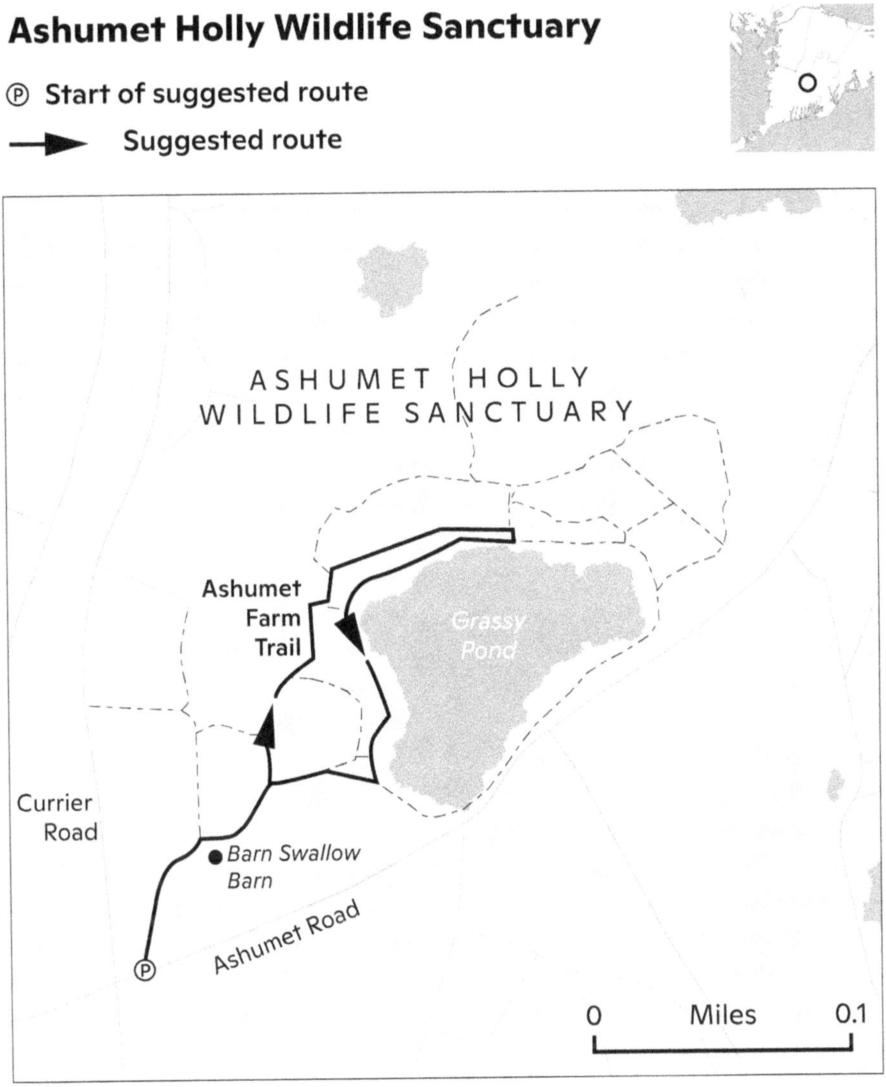

# Ashumet Holly Wildlife Sanctuary

ⓟ Start of suggested route
➡ Suggested route

firm, who then donated the property to the Audubon Society. (Mr. Lilly also purchased the Beebe Woods property near downtown Falmouth and gifted it to the town.) Many migratory birds, including Baltimore Orioles and Barn Swallows, nest on the Ashumet property. Five small vernal pools were recently dug in the hopes of attracting the threatened Eastern Spadefoot Toad.

## DIRECTIONS AND PARKING

Enter "Ashumet Holly Wildlife Sanctuary" into your navigation app. The grass parking lot is east of the intersection of Currier and Ashumet Roads, just north of Route 151. Admission is free for Audubon members but $3 per adult and $2 per child for nonmembers.

## HUNTING

Hunting is not allowed.

# SALT POND & SHINING SEA BIKEWAY

Elizabeth Saito

*The Shining Sea Bikeway runs twelve miles along an old railroad line from Woods Hole to North Falmouth.*

**Length:** 2.3 miles
**Time:** ~1 hr

**A stroll through coastal thicket and along Vineyard Sound**

## THE HIKE

This hike combines a stroll through coastal thicket with a jaunt down and back along the Shining Sea Bikeway. The coastal thicket is nestled between the bikeway and Salt Pond. Shrubs and trees grow dense enough to form archways overhead. The wide, flat trails are good for walkers of all abilities. The wheelchair-friendly bikeway section of the hike parallels the shoreline of Vineyard Sound, which is a great spot for a picnic.

Molly Johnston

*Straight-trunked red cedar trees, a native species of juniper, flank the paths through Salt Pond's coastal thicket. The bark of red cedars is reddish brown and peels easily in thin, vertical strips.*

## THE LAND

A railroad line running from the Cape Cod Canal down to Woods Hole was built in 1872 and continued to carry freight and passengers until the last train from New York rumbled through in 1964. On April 2, 1969, Falmouth town meeting voted to take the 3.1 miles of abandoned track between Locust Street and Woods Hole by eminent domain. The railroad then announced it had sold the line the day before the vote. After a six-year legal battle that went all the way to the state's Supreme Court, the town prevailed. Falmouth resident Barbara Burwell was instrumental in the town's continued fight for the bike path. Ms. Burwell's son, David Burwell—who remembers bouncing his Schwinn bicycle down the

# Salt Pond

Ⓟ  Start of suggested route
──▶  Suggested route

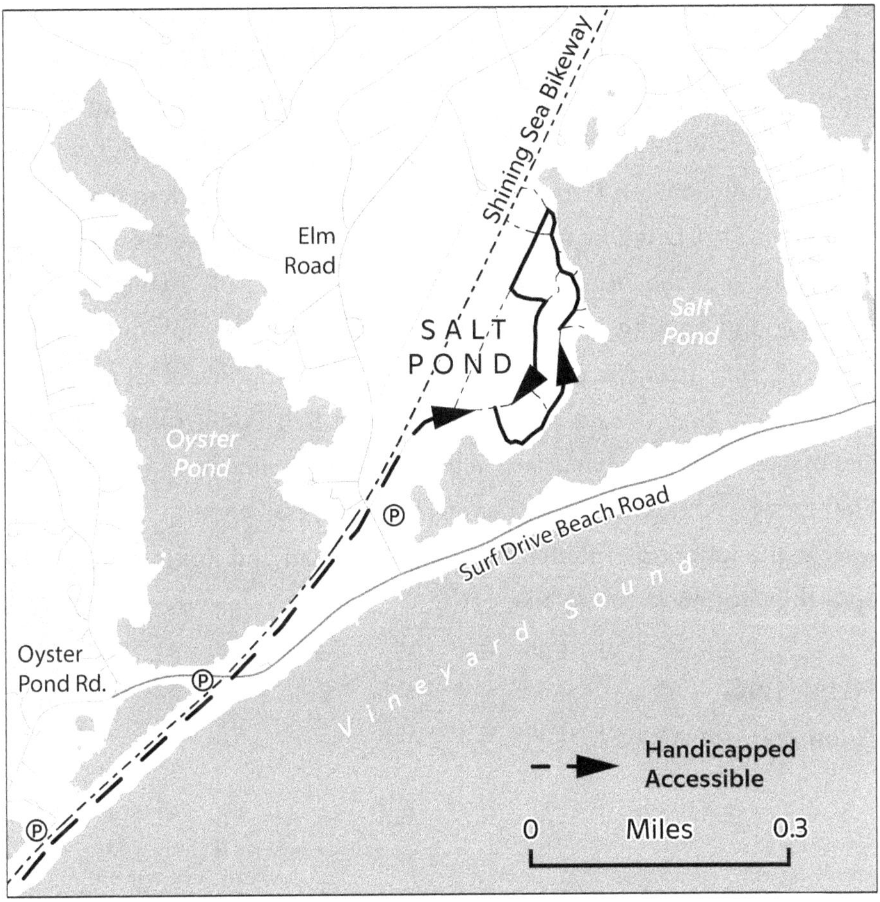

tracks to play baseball in Woods Hole—founded the national Rails-to-Trails Conservancy in 1986. The group has since converted over 24,000 miles of railroad lines into recreation trails.

In the 1960s, conservationist Ermine Lovell cobbled together forty-one acres of open space surrounding Salt Pond by soliciting donations from adjacent landowners. The land was initially transferred to the Massachusetts Audubon Society. Lovell then founded the Salt Pond

Areas Bird Sanctuaries, Falmouth's first land trust, which took over ownership of the property. Both swans and ospreys nest along the pond's perimeter.

## DIRECTIONS AND PARKING

Enter "Elm Road" into your navigation app. There is a small gravel lot a few hundred yards north of Elm Road's intersection with Surf Drive Beach Road. Walk north on the bike path, keeping an eye out for the wooden trail kiosk on the right. Alternatively, you can park in the diagonal lot on Surf Drive Beach Road just west of its intersection with the bike path, or at the Trunk River lot off Oyster Pond Road, which has two handicapped parking spaces. All three lots are usually full in the summertime. Bicyclists can park at the less crowded municipal lot off Depot Avenue, and bike the 1.2 miles south to the Salt Pond trailhead. If the Depot Ave lot is full, parking is almost always available at Mullen–Hall Elementary School, which is a short ride to the bike path via the crosswalk at the junction of Katharine Lee Bates Road and Route 28, where a spur then connects to the bike path.

## HUNTING

Hunting is not allowed.

# MARES POND & SPECTACLE POND RESERVATION

Elizabeth Saito

*Like all Cape Cod ponds, Spectacle Pond is fed from groundwater rather than a river.*

**Length:** 1.4 miles
**Time:** ~35 min

### Pine needle-coated paths crisscross undulating woodland

## THE HIKE

This loop follows a meandering course through dry, pleasant woodland. The trails are wide and clear, often flanked by towering white pines. Two offshoots lead down to the shorelines of Mares and Spectacle Ponds, where the views south over the ponds are especially lovely on a sunny winter day.

Elizabeth Saito

*White pines dominate the forest around Mares and Spectacle Ponds. White and pitch pines are the two most common pine species on the Cape. The needles of white pines grow in clusters of five, and pitch pines grow in clusters of three.*

## THE LAND

Unlike the steep, boulder-studded slopes of the town's western lands, the gently rolling hills of Mares Pond and Spectacle Pond Reservation (and the town's eastern lands generally) were formed by streams of meltwater pouring off a massive continental glacier at the end of the last ice age. The glacier reached its southernmost limit just below Cape Cod, plowing up the rocky western and northern highlands of the Cape before retreating roughly 18,000 years ago as the world warmed. These steep, rocky highlands are called moraines. The meltwater pouring down from the moraines carried silt, sand, and fine gravel, which the glacier had scraped up into itself on its long journey down from Canada. The streams flowing east and south were not powerful enough to carry the large rocks trapped in the ice sheet, which plunked straight down and

# Mares Pond Reservation

Ⓟ Start of suggested route

➤ Suggested route

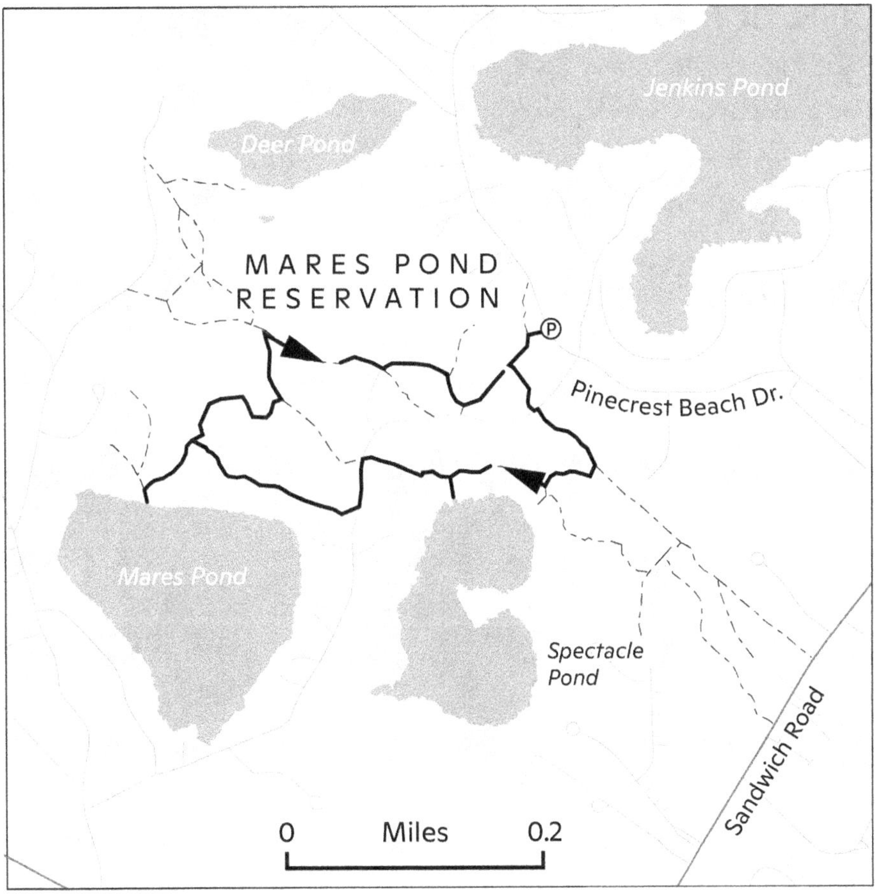

piled up into moraines. The sandy and relatively flat land comprising the Upper Cape's southeastern quadrant is known as an outwash plain.

A large water tower stands on the property. Water from a municipal well dug down into the water table is pumped up into the tower, where passive pressure then pushes the water toward homes and up faucets. Between 1986 and 2002, Falmouth acquired 152 acres of woodland surrounding the well to protect its drinking water. Forests act as natural filters, cleansing groundwater flowing toward the well; and land left undeveloped means that many fewer septic systems and herbicide-treated lawns leaching toxins into the ground.

## DIRECTIONS AND PARKING

Enter "Mares Pond and Spectacle Pond Reservation" into your navigation app. Parking is in a grassy pull-off on the south side of the Pinecrest Beach Drive just west of Owls Nest Road. A narrow trail leads from the parking area into the forest.

## HUNTING

Hunting is permitted. See page xii for details on hunting seasons.

## PETERSON FARM

Tom Noonan

*The town of Falmouth leases Peterson Farm (at no cost) to sheep farmers to preserve grassland habitat and maintain historic, pastoral vistas. Without sheep grazing them, the fields would be quickly overrun with invasive plants and poison ivy.*

**Length:** 0.6 miles
**Time:** ~15 min

**A short walk around pasture and along a wooded ridgeline**

## THE HIKE

Peterson Farm is an eighty-eight–acre conservation area with twelve acres of gently rolling pasture land and seventy-six acres of woodland. This hike takes you around the perimeter of the main pasture with a detour into the woods for a short jaunt along a ridgeline that abuts a freshwater marsh. It's a great hike for small children, especially in springtime when there's a chance of seeing newborn lambs. The walk can be extended by exploring the trails that wind through the surrounding woodland and connect to the abutting 388 acres of Beebe Woods (see page 11 for a map of Beebe Woods). On the north side of the path leading west to Ice House Pond are the remains of the old farmhouse's stone foundation.

Molly Johnston

*Through the nineteenth century, the Cape's lands were severely overgrazed, leading to erosion and poor soil quality. The farm's current shepherds use a grazing technique designed to foster healthy grasslands, home to a multitude of birds, grasshoppers, butterflies, and pollinating insects.*

## THE LAND

Peterson Farm is one of the oldest farms on Cape Cod. The land was granted to John Weeks in 1679 and farmed by the Weeks family for the next two and a half centuries. The Weeks raised cattle and sheep and maintained orchards and cropland. Wool was the primary source of income for most of the farm's history, so when demand for wool declined in the late 1800s, family members turned to other occupations. The Peterson family bought the farm in 1944 and grew corn, lettuce, tomatoes, herbs, blueberries, and strawberries, which they served to guests at their family-run hotel, the Cape Codder. The Petersons sold the farm to the town in 1998.

# Peterson Farm

ⓟ Start of suggested route
➡ Suggested route

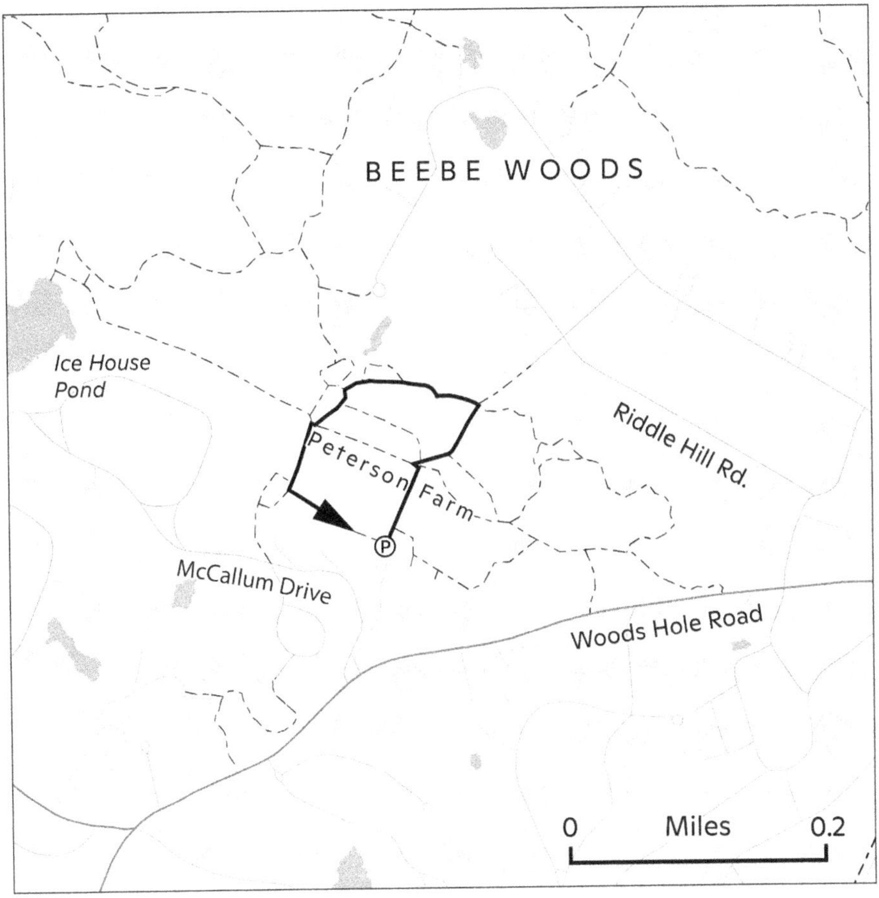

For the next twenty years, a local veterinarian raised sheep on the property, using the flock to train competition-level sheep dogs. In 2018, after a sheepless year at the farm, a robotics engineer and a marine ecologist from the Woods Hole Oceanographic Institution—both devoted sheep dog trainers—teamed up to bring in a new flock. The scientist–shepherds use a pasture management system known as rotational grazing, whereby the pasture is divided into half-acre paddocks and the sheep are rotated through them. Rotational grazing is more work for farmers, who must continually ferry interior electric fencing about their fields, but it enhances soil quality and farm productivity in the long run. After the Peterson sheep are shorn in the spring, their fleeces are shipped to custom mills in the Midwest that process the fleece into wool and stuff it into duvets. Lambs are sent to a slaughterhouse in Westport, Massachusetts, that meets the USDA's highest standard for animal welfare. The meat, tanned hides, and wool filled comforters are then sold locally.

## DIRECTIONS AND PARKING

Enter "Peterson Farm" into your phone's navigation app. The access road to the farm splinters off McCallum Drive one hundred feet beyond its intersection with Woods Hole Road. Continue up the access road until you come to a small parking lot next to the sheep barn. Do *not* attempt to access Peterson Farm from the bike path: biking along Woods Hole Road is dangerous.

## HUNTING

Hunting is not allowed.

## About the Author

Elizabeth Saito is the editor of the *Falmouth Enterprise*. Her book of essays chronicling life during the first year of the COVID-19 pandemic, *Notes from a Pandemic*, is available on Amazon and at Eight Cousins bookstore on Main Street in Falmouth. She lives near Oyster Pond with her husband, a scientist at the Woods Hole Oceanographic Institution, and their two boys.

www.ingramcontent.com/pod-product-compliance
Lightning Source LLC
Chambersburg PA
CBHW050445010526
44118CB00013B/1692